THE GOLDEN TICKET

An Honest, Easy to Read Guide on Financial
Planning, Debt Control, Investments
and Insurance for Canadians

Written by

Aaron Vissia, CFP®

With

Holly Van Schouwen, RHU

Order this book online at www.trafford.com
or email orders@trafford.com

Most Trafford titles are also available at major online book retailers.

Printed in Victoria, BC, Canada.

ISBN: 978-1-4251-8623-4

www.aaronvissia.com

*Our mission is to efficiently provide the world's finest, most comprehensive
book publishing service, enabling every author to experience success.
To find out how to publish your book, your way, and have it available
worldwide, visit us online at www.trafford.com/10510*

Trafford rev. 2/16/2010

 www.trafford.com

North America & international
toll-free: 1 888 232 4444 (USA & Canada)
phone: 250 383 6864 ♦ fax: 812 355 4082

TABLE OF CONTENTS

ACKNOWLEDGMENTS

Aaron Vissia, CFP Professional

To my wife for showing me love and devotion at every turn, and supporting me in all of our successes and failures.

To my children for showing me just how quickly time slips by when you're having fun.

To London Life for giving me my start in this career and being there to help me build my business.

My home town, the Alberni Valley, B.C. for providing me with an amazing place to grow up, raise my family, and share the good news about financial freedom.

My business network for helping elevate my business to where it is today; without all of you, I would still be struggling.

My former associate and Office Manager, Holly Van Schouwen. If it were not for her assisting me in putting these words on paper, this book would have never been made.

INTRODUCTION

With headlines screaming at us to start planning for our future financial health, and with social programs and pension plans being depleted at an alarming rate, we know that it is in all of our best interests to make a plan, stick with it, and reap the benefits now and well into the future.

With all of the options available to potential investors, and all of the various consultants, advisors and planners wanting to draw in more clients, people are wary of putting all of their eggs in one basket and listening to one source for all their financial planning advice. It seems like you need a "Golden Ticket" to succeed today. With the recent market losses and large financial company collapses in the US, making solid plans for the future seems impossible.

This book was created after realizing that while people have access to infinite information about funds, planning, and insurance, they don't know how to translate all of it into a usable plan that works. It is well known that we should all lower our debt but how do you do that when the credit keeps coming and the bills keep mounting up? We hope to help answer some basic questions and get individuals on track to achieving their dreams and goals, no matter what stage of life they are in.

CHAPTER 1

A Story about the Jones Family

Once upon a time in a town just like yours, there lived a family of 4. Bob Jones, his lovely wife Rita, and their two children, Mia, age 10, and Alexandra, age 6.

Bob grew up in a middle class family and enjoyed the privilege of attending university after high school all paid for by his hardworking blue collar parents. Upon graduation from university, Bob was hired as an engineer with a municipality and his future looked rosy and bright as he received a handsome salary and benefits package. He met Rita shortly after beginning his career and they married within two years. Rita came from a lower income family and worked as a retail sales person in the early years of their marriage.

With just the two of them initially, their financial picture looked good as their expenses were considerably lower than the income coming in each month. They were young and enjoying life with frequent trips away together, gatherings with friends and colleagues from Bob's work, and planning what their lives would look like in the years to come. Rita kept her earnings for herself as Bob brought in more than ample income and he felt it was his sole responsibility to care for his family. Within 3 years, Rita became pregnant with Mia, and the Jones family was set to expand and change.

The couple sat down together and discussed what they wanted for their child and how they wanted their life to look. Bob had recently received a raise and they decided that now was the time to purchase a house. As Bob's co-workers spoke highly about a subdivision going into a new part of town, and Rita had big plans for designing the interior based on a magazine she ordered, he went to the bank to determine what he could borrow. The house that they looked at (a show home as the dwelling they wanted was not yet created) made Rita cry with joy. Wanting to make a good impression and appear successful, Bob signed the papers for a mortgage that included monthly payments of almost triple the current rent that they were paying. He didn't feel it necessary to discuss it with Rita as he was sure he would continue to do well at work and he didn't want to burst her bubble.

The house was done just before the baby was born, but as is usually the case, Bob needed to take out a line of credit to pay for the unexpected costs of designing the interior as Rita wanted. He rationalized that he could cover the costs until Rita went back to work and then they could pay it off in full.

Upon Mia's arrival, the Jones' held a large party to welcome her and show off their prosperity with the brand new dwelling. Guest after guest approached the couple and gushed at the house and how beautiful each room was. Bob felt great that night, as though he had truly accomplished something awesome. Rita was glowing in the praise, and again the future looked bright. They both remarked to each other that this night was what life is all about.

Not long after, Bob's parents came by to see them and offer Rita a hand with the baby. After a gourmet dinner (catered by a well known local *establishment because Rita wanted time to look just right), Bob and his father sat down to talk. Bob's father remarked at the size of the house and the many furnishings they had purchased. He cautioned Bob on having too much too soon and asked him if he was saving for the family's future. Bob became immediately offended at his father's remark and explained that he was setting the trend amongst his peers and because his job was going so well, he was not concerned for the future. The economy was great and he expected that his yearly raises and bonuses would more than cover all of the expenses. His father slowly shook his head and sighed.*

A year or so after Mia was born, Bob received a promotion at work that included travel and a more public role within the organization. Feeling on top of the world, he and Rita sat down after a celebratory dinner with 20 of his closest friends and again discussed their future. Because he wanted to make a good impression with his bosses and colleagues, he felt that Rita should not go back to work but stay at home with Mia. He explained that he wanted Rita to have it all—be free to keep the house as she pleased, host functions and gatherings that would bolster his career, take up hobbies that she was interested in, and set themselves as an example of success to everyone that they met. Having not had much when growing up, Rita was overjoyed. Visions of parties and get togethers set amongst perfectly designed backdrops and expensive dresses filled her mind.

"This is what the good life is," she thought to herself.

She was proud to be Bob's wife and wanted everyone to know how successful he was.

As usually happens at the 5 year mark, the family car needed repair and the bill was going to be costly. With Bob now taking business associates out more frequently and Rita involved in many different societies and groups, he decided that they each needed a new vehicle. He required an expensive SUV to wow his peers and provide safety on those long trips away, and Rita needed something that made her look good amongst the society wives she associated with, not to mention the need to keep Mia protected.

Interest rates were low and he decided that purchasing higher-end vehicles was a sound investment for their future. The monthly payments were *almost two thirds of their mortgage payment but Bob wanted to pay for quality.*

Now in their mid thirties, Rita became pregnant again with Alexandra and everyone was excited. Rita used a debit card to make all of the family's purchases. She traveled with a friend to an expensive design studio to begin planning for the new baby's room. After settling on furnishings and décor, Rita gave the card to the salesman to ring through the required deposit. She browsed some more and the clerk called her to the register. He asked her if she had another card she could use, as the current card showed nonsufficient funds. Her face went white and her stomach turned. Quietly she told the clerk that she would have to come back, and murmured an apology. Suddenly laughing, she took her friend by the arm and exclaimed that she had brought the wrong card by mistake. They left and she laughed about the "mistake" over lunch.

Bob was not expected home until the weekend and she didn't want to bother him on the road, so she waited, avoiding her usual tennis match and social outings for the week. She knew what it was like not to have money and didn't want anyone to know.

When Bob arrived home late Friday night, he was visibly tired and drained which seemed to be more and more the case lately. After preparing him a drink, she sat down and took a deep breath. She explained that a "mistake" had occurred while she was shopping and did he know what happened? Bob sat upright with a start and immediately questioned her on who she may have told about the mistake. Rita explained that no one knew, and now somewhat worried, she asked if everything was okay. Bob suddenly shifted his weight and with a big smile told her everything was fine.

"Go back to the store on Monday," he said, "I forgot to transfer over some funds; it won't happen again."

With that, he got up, embraced Rita and went upstairs to bed. As seemed to be more and more frequent, Bob lay awake most of the night thinking about his next meeting, the next event, and how impressed people were with the life he had built.

"This is what the good life is," he assured himself, "people want to be me, so I must have it all".

Alexandra was born, many parties ensued, and soon the girls were in school. Rita found herself growing bored at home and discontented with her prized social calendar. She reminisced about her childhood. She recalled that when things were tight at home her family spent more time talking and sharing books and stories with each other to pass the time. She loved those memories and remembered when her parents took her and her siblings for their first vacation.

Having little money to spare for extras her parents borrowed a tent from the neighbours and set it up in their small backyard. For 10 days that summer, the family vacationed in the backyard, playing, laughing, and roasting marshmallows until the early hours of the morning.

"We have more money and friends now than I ever had growing up," she thought, "so why does it feel like I have nothing now?"

She was determined to bring the same joy and togetherness to her family but found it hard to communicate with Bob very much at all lately. He was angry and irritable almost all of the time, when he was actually home, and rumors among her social circles were that the economy was taking a turn for the worse. Of course whenever this was brought up, the laughter was light and the ladies always assured themselves that they were beyond the problems that a bad economy could bring.

Now approaching 40, Bob arrived home late one evening to find Rita's tear stained face looking up at him from the dining room table. Feeling exhausted himself, he considered heading straight to bed and forgetting that his wife was in tears. He wearily pulled out a beautiful leather dining chair and sat down beside her. Sighing, he softly asked her what was wrong. Rita burst into tears and between sobs he made out that the bank had called earlier to say that they were behind on their mortgage payments. The representative asked that they have the back payments to the branch by the next week. Rita sobbed that she thought they were beyond the problems that "regular" people have with money, and wanted to know what was going on.

Upon hearing the words "regular people", Bob became stiff and in a strong unwavering voice said, "Rita, we are the Jones'; we are beyond regular people. People look to us as an example of success. I don't know how this mistake happened, but don't worry, it will be fixed tomorrow."

Slowly he rose from the table, patted her lovingly on the head and went upstairs to bed. Rita rose too and following Bob to the stairs she called "Bob, are we in trouble, is everything going to be okay?"

Bob turned around and gazed down at her,

"Honey, it's just a mistake, look around you, does it look like we are in trouble?" With that, he set off to bed, another sleepless night ahead of him.

Not long after, Rita was sitting at her kitchen table watching the maid clean up after breakfast. She had mentioned to Rita that she needed time off to spend with her family for summer vacation. Rita agreed and asked what her plans were. The maid shyly replied,

"Well, we don't have the resources that you do madam, but I thought that we could spend the time together exploring the town on our bikes."

With that she went about cleaning the stove, leaving Rita to think about what was said.

Bob was never home now and the girls were involved in so many activities that she never saw anyone in her family it seemed. A feeling of jealousy overtook her and she proceeded upstairs to fix herself up for her afternoon shopping excursion with friends. While getting ready, thought after thought invaded her mind, "This is not what the good life is; why can't I be happy?", other evil notions crept in.

When Rita returned in the afternoon, her vehicle was gone from its pad in front of the house. Startled, she ran inside and phoned the dealership. Putting on her best face, she politely asked the dealer if the car was in the shop for detailing and when she should pick it up. Her face fell when the dealer remarked that they had sent numerous messages and mail to the house about the car. Payments for the vehicle were overdue and had not been paid for almost 3 months. Rita thanked the dealer and softly told him that her husband would take care of it. She hung up the phone and stared blankly out the kitchen window. Her husband always had the mail directed to himself and she rarely saw any of it unless it was an invitation or request for her to host another fancy get together.

Remembering where she had seen him put important paperwork in his den, she went to the desk drawer and opened it up. She felt guilty about looking at her husband's papers but felt an over-whelming need to find out what was going on. Opening the cabinet she gasped at the number of unopened envelopes that were inside. She picked some up and noticed words like PAST DUE and IMMEDIATE ATTENTION REQUIRED staring at her like an intruder. She made the decision to open up the letters and was shocked at the contents. The luxuries and necessities that she had taken for granted throughout the years were threatened to be taken away very soon. Putting the envelopes back in the cabinet, she closed the door and made a very hard choice.

It was later that year, the weekend of Thanksgiving that Bob came home weary from his latest trip abroad. Lately, his thoughts were consumed by the feeling that he was living someone else's life and living up to someone else's expectations of him. Happy to be home, he entered the house expecting to hear the sounds of his children laughing and getting ready for the lavish turkey dinner he had come to expect each year. The stale silence throughout the house was deafening. Putting his coat and briefcase down, he walked into the kitchen wondering where his family was.

"Perhaps I missed the message that dinner was going to be held elsewhere this year," he thought.

Moving to the counter with the phone, he was about to call his wife on her cell when an envelope propped up against the counter caught his eye. Immediately recognizing his wife's handwriting, he opened the letter. As he began to read, the phone rang and startled, he dropped the letter.

About a half hour later, Bob hung up the phone and felt like his chest was tightening down, threatening to crush his spirit as well as his lungs. The office had called.

Due to a change in management and a new direction for the municipality, Bob had lost his job. Trying to sugar coat the bad news, his boss explained that he would receive a handsome six figure compensation package but all his retirement benefits were lost. Not wanting to appear weak, Bob said thank you, wondering how the package could be spread thin enough to pay for his mounting bills. The package was only a quarter of his current outstanding mortgage and with his monthly expenses so high, there was no way he could avoid telling his family and would be forced to admit that he was not as successful as everyone thought he was.

Suddenly, he remembered the letter and picked it up. Soon he realized that he did not have to tell his family, they already knew.

Rita and the girls were gone and not coming back. He wondered if it was because of the car fiasco that had happened awhile back, but he had that all straightened out. He went to a new bank and took out a loan to cover the missed payments. His brain swimming, he went to his office and sat defeated at his desk.

"How did this all go so wrong?" he thought to himself, "We had everything anyone would want and yet here I am left with nothing."

CHAPTER 2

Setting & Understanding Priorities

Many books, seminars, and infomercials offer advice and insight on planning your financial future. Most have some valuable advice hidden within the pages, "if you can get past the fluff", and industry jargon. Our hope with this book is that it will provide to you valuable advice and a template for you to use in creating your own vision of financial security and success.

Setting Priorities

Priority #1

Wills & Power of Attorney

Before you begin to plan your financial success story, make sure you have the proper cornerstones in place. Regardless of whether you are married with children, single, or divorced, if you are over 18, YOU NEED A WILL.

This document is literally the roadmap that the loved ones you leave behind will use to determine what you wanted to see happen after you pass away. Without this roadmap, the government determines where your assets go based on the guidelines in your province.

We know of an individual who met his untimely demise recently that is a perfect illustration of what can go wrong when you do not have a will or do not keep your life insurance beneficiary designations up to date. Names and some details have been changed out of respect.

Marcus was a successful entrepreneur who had just begun to enjoy satisfaction with his life at age 45. He had investments and insurance in place for years, and had a considerable nest egg tucked away.

While on vacation, Marcus passed away suddenly and it came time for his children to look at settling his estate. Once the kids had waded through his paperwork and records, shock and horror came upon them.

Marcus had put his insurance and investments in place many years ago while he was married and had children and then never gave the contracts a second look. His marriage had ended when he was in his 20s for various reasons but he never looked at changing the beneficiaries from his now ex wife to his present children. Marcus also never took the time to have a will drawn up.

The inevitable conclusion to this story, you can probably already guess. Marcus's ex wife received the proceeds from all of his assets and his children got nothing. There was a lengthy battle, but little the courts could do to reverse the decisions he had made years prior. KEEP YOUR WILL AND ALL INSURANCE AND INVESTMENT DOCUMENTS

CURRENT! Be sure to keep in contact with any designated "executor" and be sure he/she knows where the will/documents are, or give him/her a copy.

The other document that is equally as important is a power of attorney agreement. Should you suffer from a disorder or ailment that renders it impossible for you to act on your own behalf with financial, health and legal matters you need to have an individual that you trust ready to handle the potential issues for you. Take time to select the right person(s) to take on this role. There have been many instances where abuses of this role have caused serious problems for the individual that bestowed the trust in the first place, so discuss this with your family, trusted friends, and legal professionals.

Priority #2

Debt And Budgeting

Almost everyone we know wants to be debt free, have a sizable nest egg, and the security of knowing everything will be alright, now and in the future. Everyone seems to have this vision for themselves but few actually put the dream into an action plan to make it a reality. If you are starting this book and are not ready to take the hard line for yourself, hopefully in reading on, you will see the importance of knowing the basics and become committed to ensuring your success.

You may be familiar with the phrase "Pay yourself first" coined by a well known financial analyst. This phrase is so timely for today's constantly changing marketplace and applies to all areas of financial planning.

We are beginning to become more aware that we alone will be responsible for funding our future, retirement, medical and health services, and even estate costs. The number one action that must be taken to ensure that you and your family are taken care of is to put yourself and your future needs first.

Many people say they will plan for retirement tomorrow or when they have some money. If you are working, you have some money now. It is a shame that we are so bombarded by TV and other media to spend, spend, spend now, and worry about financing and costs later. We believe that we live in an age of self-entitlement in which we are under the wrong assumption that we deserve to own everything we ever dream of now. If you don't have the money, borrow it, re-finance the house, put it on credit—you deserve it now!

Our country's founding fathers will tell you, we are sure, that virtually no one had everything all at once when they were working to shape the country. The same goes for working to plan a life for yourself.

If you vacation every year with borrowed money while you are working, you will never vacation in your retirement years. You will still be working to pay back all the previous vacations that are beginning to fade from memory.

This is not to say that you cannot enjoy yourself and reap some of the benefits of your income now. What we are saying is do everything in moderation. It falls back to the need-vs-want issue. So much of our time is consumed by spending and working to spend, that we think we are missing out on the finer things in life such as family time, walks, conversations with loved ones, and enjoying nature. We have rooked ourselves into believing that you need money to do anything of any meaning, and this is simply not true.

Honestly, it's all about balance.

Finances (spending) need to be in balance with your current income. If you are feeling that your income is too low, you need to find a way to increase your income. How do I find income in my current job, you may be asking. Each of us as adults has choices in life. We are all empowered with being able to make our own decisions. If you feel that you are stuck in your current position, then chances are you will remain stuck there. YOU need to expand your horizons and think outside "your" box, beyond what you think is possible. Will this be easy? Of course not, if it were we would all be riding high on the gravy train, but we aren't. It's those of us who make that extra effort to better ourselves that will generally reap the rewards.

As an example, let's go back to the Jones'. Had Bob & Rita made an extra effort at starting some kind of home-based business for Rita instead of putting themselves on a pedestal to look better to those around them, three important aspects of their lives would have changed:

1. Rita would have been more involved in the input of family finances and income, and

2. Rita would have achieved the feeling of self-accomplishment, rather than loneliness and boredom, and

3. that home based business could have grown into something which would have protected the Jones family when Bob lost his position.

You may not look so good to others today, but you will look great to your family and when it's time to retire, you will look like a million bucks.

Ask yourself what you would look like in 10 years if you earned $3,000 per month but spent $4,000. Let's not even factor in interest rates, in 10 years forgetting any other expenses or debts, you would owe over $120,000! This is equal to approximately 3 ½ years of income. How do you ever escape this? This is why balance in life and with your finances is so important, so you and your family don't end up like the Jones family did.

Any good business plan, project, or other undertaking takes hard work, dedication, and discipline. We must apply this principal to our financial lives as well as other aspects in order to realize true success for ourselves. A willingness to sit down and objectively look at your current situation is key to making the first action step of paying yourself first happen.

Once you have come to the decision that you need to organize your financial affairs and start a definitive plan for the future, regardless of where you are at in life, you need to ask yourself and/or your family some hard questions and be willing to look critically at your monthly income and expenditures. Included in this book is a sample expense and budget sheet with valuable tools in determining what your financial picture looks like now, and where you can make changes for your future. See page 132 for the sample Expense Work Sheet.

Don't be surprised if you don't like the initial results that you get when you have completed the monthly budget expense sheet and find that you are overspending. This is a common occurrence for many Canadians today.

Monthly Budget Sheet

This tool is very user friendly and if filled in accurately and truthfully will give you an accurate snapshot of where your income goes each month. Be sure to sit down with your spouse or partner if applicable when doing this to ensure that all areas are accounted for and used for your totals. We have provided an example on page 133 at the end of the book.

When most people complete a worksheet like this, they are surprised to see how much money actually gets spent in a month. Having this record on paper increases the sense of importance and urgency to be diligent in spending wisely and within your means and/or knowing how to increase your means.

When you have completed the expense portion of the worksheet, input the total in the designated box at the bottom. Now, input your total net household income (income in hand after deductions) and subtract your expenses from your income. If the result is negative, you will need to take a hard look at where your income is going every month and immediately make adjustments accordingly.

There are two kinds of expenses in every monthly balance sheet: fixed costs and variable costs.

Fixed costs are things such as rent, mortgage payments, car payments, loan payments, insurance premiums, property tax and any other monthly/yearly obligations that you cannot change the payment price of.

Variable costs are virtually everything else. Things such as food, entertainment, personal care, and travel costs are the big ones in this category. Costs like hydro, cable, phone, and gas are also considered variable because while there is a set base rate, the costs can be controlled by minimizing use of these when the bills get too high. This can happen in the winter months.

I've completed the expense sheet and I'm in the red and not getting ahead, now what?

Once you have honestly completed the exercise and are looking at the hard facts of your financial picture, take some time to let the truth of your reality sink in.

For many who have been letting bills and past due notices pile up, it can be an emotional experience to look squarely at your problems and confront them. Talk with your spouse about what you see and how you feel about the current situation. By reacting honestly to the truth and sharing it with those involved, you will almost instantly feel better about getting rid of the debt and letting go of the load that has been with you.

For many, as soon as they have completed the exercise, ideas on how to reduce expenses and debt begin to pop into their minds. When you force your mind to view things from an honest perspective and accept that change needs to be made, your brain begins to create solutions for you and gives you the initial strength to go through the process of change.

Like making any hard change such as quitting smoking, sticking to a diet, or starting a new career, it won't be easy to change habits overnight. You will need to be strong in your resolve to stick with the plans you create and have rewards in place when you have success-fully stuck to your budget for a decent period of time, such as 6 months. More about setting goals and rewarding yourself is mentioned later on in this chapter.

The next step in becoming debt free, or learn-ing to live within your means and save for your future goals and plans, is to reduce the variable costs for a given month and/or look at ways of increasing income.

One of the first places to look to make these adjustments is the area of Food and Entertainment. Weekly trips to restaurants add up quickly as does entertainment. Be sure to include liquor costs in this area as well. Almost everyone can find a way to shave off a few dol-lars in this category. Another area to look at when trying to cut back on spending is Cable, Clothing, and Gasoline.

In our area of Canada full cable costs amount to over $100 per month, while basic cable is ap-prox. $30. Gasoline continues to rise in price with no signs of stopping, so if you commute to work or travel long distances for employ-ment, look at driving less on weekends/off time to conserve funds and vehicle wear and tear, or consider a carpool.

The conveniences of modern society have become mandatory for many families and individuals and most cannot dream of not being able to watch their favorite specialty channels each night. Imagine having to read a book or tend to yard work that you have neglected instead of settling in for an evening of prime time television. Change your thought patterns now or your brain will try to go back to old habits and provide you with a million excuses to put off the necessary adjustments in your life.

We have actually heard some individuals ask if it is possible to be happy while doing an activity that doesn't cost money.

To them we say, "Are you serious?" Have we come such a long way since the industrial age and now into the information age that we can't find joy and satisfaction from enjoying the simple things like stopping to smell the roses?

Don't buy into this misconception fed to us by various media and consumer product providers. The more that we clog up our lives and thoughts with the need to consume and spend, the more disgruntled with life we become and our satisfaction with life in general goes downhill.

How many people do you know that are taking some sort of antidepressant because they aren't happy and feel like life is slipping away in front of them? Perhaps it is you? Not to say that everyone suffering from depression on some level has money problems and by cleaning up their finances everything will begin to get better. But really, do you think by keeping up with the Jones family and desiring what everyone tells you that you need will make you happy?

CHAPTER 3

Good Debt & Bad Debt

Everyone has a different opinion about what types of debt are actually good for your long term financial plan and those that are not. There are many publications available that illustrate in depth the various forms but for the purpose of basic planning we have compiled a brief list, and explanations for your information and discussion with an advisor or planner.

BAD DEBT

1. Credit Cards/High Interest Loans

This can be for boats, furniture, electronics and appliances that you do not immediately need.

It does not take an expert to know that having balances owing on credit cards and high interest loans are bad debt. It is so easy to pull out the plastic and make a purchase that you and your family don't really need right now, but hey, it's on sale and you can pay it off next month. So many individuals get caught up in this buy today, pay tomorrow mentality and when the statement comes in, they are shocked at the balance and wonder how it ever got that high. The answer to solving this is obvious, pay with cash only and CUT UP THE CARD! **Follow the golden rule of spending: If you don't have the money to pay off the full balance at the end of the month, then don't use the card and don't make the purchase!**

High interest loans are usually the result of borrowing money with bad credit or paying off a credit card balance. Inquire with your lender about obtaining a better interest rate after a year of consistent payments, or double up your pay-

ments to bring the principal (amount originally owing) down more quickly.

2. New Car Payments/Loans

I would imagine that dealerships everywhere do not want to see this part published, but let's face it. A car IS a liability. Rarely do you see a car appreciate or gain in value, more often you see it decrease. Again, I believe that people get caught up in the idea that having that shiny new sports car or SUV will make them happy or look good.

An example from Holly:

I have personally gone through this twice. I bought a near-new sports car that I had always wanted. The price was a bit high but I figured I was living out my dream and the value that I placed on the vehicle would far outweigh the black book value. After driving around all summer long, fall came and with it the frost and cold. My new sports car was rendered useless for my commute to work, (not to mention that I had more then doubled my fuel cost and maintenance). I was forced to take the car off the road for 6 months and park it.

When spring came along and after long family discussions about it, it was determined that the sports car was just not feasible for daily use. I went to a local dealership to inquire about trading it in for a more practical vehicle and thought that the trade in value should be close to what I paid, as I had only driven the car for 5 months. THINK AGAIN! I was livid when the salesman came to me without a smile and offered me 33% of what I had paid for it. Needless to say, I lost on that transaction in more ways than one. I often suggest to people now that if they are in the market for a new car, spend at least 2 months doing research on the type of car you want, the prices for new vs. used, and the known costs for maintenance and repairs. Make sure you aren't caught within the trap of depreciation! Most individuals and families do not need a NEW car, just a car that is new to YOU.

Let's look at a better way to purchase that shiny new vehicle.

First, set a goal for the car that you have been dreaming about having. Inquire responsibly about the true cost. For illustration purposes we will use $30,000 as an example. If you go out and buy that car today your payment will be $608 per month based on an 8% interest rate. Over the five years you will have paid $36,480 for that car and remember it is now 5 years old and worth only $10,000-$15,000.

If you set your goal to buy this car in 5 years, start making monthly payments of $350 today into a short term investment earning 4% interest. You will have saved $19,224!! Now go out and pay cash for that new car! The dealership is happy having made the sale, and you are happy with your realized goal.

The only loser in this deal is the financing company.

Debt and Debt Reduction

Average total Canadian household debt is currently equivalent to 121% of disposable income, up from 86% in 1980. Mortgage and consumer debt alone are equal to 105% of disposable income, up 31% from 1980. Low interest rates have made this debt level manageable for most families but many will be in trouble when interest rates rise. More than 79,218 Canadians declared bankruptcy in 2006. What exactly are we teaching ourselves and our children?

Canadians are spending more on everything, from medical drugs and recreation to education and entertainment. Total spending increased almost 30% per household from 1980 to 2004 while after-tax incomes increased just 4%. Analysis by household age groups reveals that, by far, the groups that bear the greatest financial burden are 25-34 and 35-44 years. They have seen their household net worth decrease 36% and 18% respectively.

As most financial planners will tell you, reducing debt as soon as possible will go a long way to improving your future financial outlook. Go over your debt obligations and make a conscientious choice to pay down the highest interest rate debt first. If you are faced with numerous bills and payments due or overdue, meet with a debt counselor as they can work as a liaison between you and your creditors to come to an agreement about repayment terms and possibly negotiate reduced interest rates. Set a realistic timeline to pay the debts and stick to it.

No one should be proud of declaring bankruptcy. This maneuver should be seen as a forbidden sin.

More Debt to stay away from.

Let's discuss what we like to call a "cancer" in the financial industry.

Any "loans until payday" type of business is out to get you. Please stay away from these types of lenders!

What you will pay as interest, which they often refer to as "fees" to make it legal, are outrageous.

Borrow $1,000 and they will charge you a fee of $20 per $100 which needs to be paid within 2 weeks. "That doesn't sound so bad," you may say, "its only 20%." WRONG!!! Let us do the math for you.

$20 per $100 from a loan of $1,000 is $200. Interest is always charged annually and you have to pay back the loan by the next pay date in 2 weeks or less. There are 26, 2 week periods in a year, so multiply 26 x 20% and the REAL interest rate becomes 520%!!

That's 520% you paid on the $1000.

The loan company earns $5,200 per annum on your $1,000. Now does it look like a "not so bad" idea? So many folks get caught in this vicious circle and will never see their way out. Don't become a statistic.

Disposable Income

If, when you total your monthly net income (take home pay after deductions) and deduct expenses and the result is not negative, you have disposable income. This is income that can be used for savings and planning for your retirement, education, vacations and other projects or goals that you have. Under the category of other, if you are currently contributing to education, registered or non-registered savings make sure that you include these in your expenses.

Before going any further, make a goals and objectives worksheet and begin to fill this out. Take your time in discussing and figuring out your personal, professional and financial goals. As always, remember to be realistic, and take all of your retirement considerations to heart. When it comes to projecting future income for yourself and/or your family, consider that you will most likely not have a mortgage, and savings will not need to be included here, provided you PLAN to be debt free in retirement.

Once you have a broad idea of the goals and dreams that you have, it is much easier to determine what course of action will take you there.

GOOD DEBT

Now it's time to talk about good debt. Good debt, is there really such a thing? ABSOLUTELY!

Good debt mainly comes in one form. It is debt that purchases assets that produce an income or have potential to produce income in the future. One good example is real estate. If you borrow to purchase a second home for rental, condo, or apartment building, these income producing assets potentially give you the ability to write off the interest payment from your taxes. As time goes by, providing your assets are properly managed, the tenants will be helping buy you your future retirement while making the debt (mortgage) payments now. Please see chapter 9 for more information or contact your financial advisor and real estate professional.

Another type of good debt is borrowing money to purchase or start a business which has the ability to produce income. This type of investment requires you to honestly know yourself, what you like, what you can do, and discover your ability to run a business or have someone that you trust run it for you.

While this is not for everyone, keep an open eye and mind for opportunities that could come your way. Of course these types of investments are not always simply done and much effort is required to be successful. If it were that easy, we would all be doing it.

To close this, we recap the following message: Good Debt buys assets that produce income, Bad Debt does not.

CHAPTER 4

Building a Working Debt reduction budget

So you know now what good and bad debt is, what your fixed and variable costs are and exactly what you are bringing in each month income wise. You have sat down with your partner and discussed the figures and reality of your situation and talked about goals you have for the short and long term.

Now its time to make a 3 month budget for the household. You can cut up all your credit cards and begin to operate on a cash only basis which is a very effective way of preventing future debt from mounting, or you can put the cards away and make the conscious choice to stop using them and begin to build rather than tear down your financial resources.

We discussed that if you have credit card debt, consumer or personal loans you may want to consolidate this debt to reduce interest payable, but this is not a choice for everyone. As a general rule, if the debt total is over $40,000, try to consolidate it. If it is under that amount, look at paying off the balances with the highest rates first. Beware of getting caught continuously refinancing your mortgage to consolidate. You are not repaying anything if the cycle of spending and lending is not stopped. The banks hook you longer by doing this, and it is their future they guarantee, not yours. As has been discussed in other chapters of this book, society is forcing the idea of drawing equity out of your house as something you deserve. We are not saying that you don't deserve anything, but the real estate market is far too volatile to be pulling so called "equity" out to vacation, renovate, or purchase a new vehicle. Also as mentioned, contact your creditors to see about reducing the interest rates if at all possible. Most will work with you to make this happen.

Look at the total net household income available to you and determine where you can cut your variable costs. Cuts to variable costs when working to become debt free can be as high as 60%, so be prepared to make some drastic changes to your grocery and entertainment bills each month.

We use a budget style that goes by each payday that occurs in a given month. As an example, if John and Jane both work full time but John gets paid biweekly and Jane gets paid bimonthly, then you will have 4 pay dates for each month's budget. Average out John's biweekly net income so that in the months where he gets paid 3 times, you can use that income to directly reduce debt. Those odd pay dates will be included in the budget for debt reduction only.

In the beginning stages you will want to be as aggressive as you can be in reducing the debts owing. If it is feasible, double up on your mortgage payments or go from monthly to accelerated biweekly payments. Allocate certain amounts for bills such as hydro and cable and pay them according to when the budget says to, don't wait for the bills to come in the mail. By paying the same amount each month at the same time it will become habit and in cases where hydro bills are less in the summer, you will establish a credit for the winter increases.

See the worksheets chapter for a sample six month budget.

Once you have adhered to a budget successfully for six months, it is time to meet with a financial planner or advisor to talk about building funds and nest eggs for education, retirement, and your other goals or be prepared to put in the time and education required to do it alone.

A financial planner or advisor can now help you to build a plan for yourself and your family. For smaller goals such as "painting the house" or "sending the kids to camp", use the common method of setting aside a specific amount of funds each month in an envelope or different bank account. Most small goals do not take more than a year to make happen and it is easier to manage this yourself than developing a sophisticated plan for the funds. Determining which type of advisor or planner that is best for you is the next area to tackle.

CHAPTER 5

Why do I need a professional advisor?

We know of a lovely lady whose personal story about "financial advisors" will resonate with all of us.

Mrs. Smith came into our office to review a plan held with us and in the course of the interview got very upset when we spoke to her about her plans held with another firm.

In her own words:

"I started accounts for my grandkids close to 10 years ago thinking that I was smart in planning to put something aside for their education or travel in their young adult lives. I sat with a gentleman who told me that was an excellent idea and he set up several accounts for me. As I am not an experienced investor, he recommended high risk mutual funds to me and I trusted his advice."

"Several years later after not hearing from him since opening the accounts, I received a statement in the mail and was shocked to see the bottom line. I had lost close to 25% on the initial investment amount for each account! I called the toll free phone number listed on my statement to enquire what was going on. After being passed through what seemed like endless representatives, I was told that my advisor would be given the message and would call me. I waited close to six weeks and had not heard anything."

As the saying goes, "Life Happened", and I forgot about this for awhile.

"Again, a few years later, I happened upon

a recent statement, and was floored as now I had lost almost 50% of my initial investment amounts! Remembering what had happened prior, I contacted the local office and asked to speak with my advisor. He no longer worked for that firm I was informed, and I was given the voice mail of a new representative who now handled my accounts. I left a message for him to contact me and still heard nothing. I tried in vain to speak with the branch manager about the situation, but he seemed indifferent and told me that I was being difficult."

"Imagine, me being difficult about my own money!"

"To this day, I have tried to reach some resolution to this, but have not had contact from the firm or its advisors. I don't know who to trust anymore, and I just don't want to think about it."

Many individual investors have a tale to tell that is pretty similar to Mrs. Smith's story. We want to start a plan and get on the train before it leaves the proverbial station so we go out and seek professional advice. With so many choices out there in the marketplace, it's hard to know who's right and who will truly look after your investments. So, you talk to friends, look in the paper, or go online and you select Advisor ABC.

Mr. ABC seems to know his stuff, he speaks with big words and talks of big growth...... so you trust him. Unfortunately, after you signed the application or transfer papers, you never really hear from him unless you call when you receive the annual statement in the mail and need someone to interpret it.

On various statements, you gain a bit, on others you lose some. You have no idea what the fund names mean or the charts and percentages, but...... you trust your advisor. Time goes by and you think, I must be doing well if Mr. ABC isn't calling, what have I got to worry about? I have invested with a professional.

In our opinion, Mr. ABC does not really hold out to be a professional with his lack of personal contact and review. While he talks big, (and probably drives a big car) he delivers small both in returns and reassurance to his clients.

The Truth about Advisors

In actual fact, no one "needs" an advisor, but many should have one. If we all had the time to research and take courses about investing, we could do it ourselves, it's not rocket science, but it would be a full time job and most of us would prefer not spending the time thinking about it.

Prior to the mid eighties, investors were considered to be the affluent and rich individuals with hoards of money to make money with. The opening up of the mutual fund market to the middle classes was done so that people would actively participate in the economy, not only as consumers but as shareholders in every industry under the sun.

As well, governments and corporations started to realize that they may not be able to sustain pension plans and income supplements to the population as they aged, so they made contributing to an investment plan attractive by adding tax incentives to them. The most common plan known as the RRSP, or Registered Retirement Savings Plan was introduced in 1971.

But as stated, having a solid working knowledge of the markets, trends, and tax implications is a full time job. Thus, the idea of the financial advisor became more mainstream to the general public.

If you are like the multitude of individual investors that do not have the time to monitor all this information and the numerous changes, you owe it to yourself to meet with a planner/advisor to work out a plan for you. The key to finding the right advisor is in asking 6 questions in the initial meeting before talking about any of your personal finances. Use these questions as a starting point for your quest for an advisor:

1. How long have you been in the business? Why did you get into the business?

I would recommend to anyone that they work with an advisor with at least 3 to 5 years experience in the field if not more. A seasoned professional will have seen the markets through ups and downs and be better equipped to help you through the volatility. Second, asking why they got into the business lets you know where their values and priorities lie when it comes to delivering the goods. If you choose to work with a new or "green" advisor, ensure that they are strongly supported and committed to continuing education. If they leave their present firm, you want to know who your account will be passed on to.

2. What is your overall investment strategy for your clients?

One of the most important questions to ask any advisor or planner is their investment strategy. Some planners invest primarily for growth while others will be more conservative looking to ensure that each individual's situation is taken into consideration. There are strict policies that advisors must follow when investing on your behalf. One of these is the Know Your Client Rule, which instructs advisors to ask you specific questions to help determine your risk tolerance, need for the money in future and current income/net worth levels.

3. How often will you meet with us for review? Will you call us with any major changes?

As illustrated with Mrs. Smith's story, it can sometimes seem that after you sign the application and your cheque is taken, you never hear from the advisor again. By asking up front what kind of service and review your potential planner will provide, you can determine some of his/her level of commitment to your plan's success. It is important to note here that advisors are in the business of making money just like everyone else and some chose to specialize in specific areas of expertise or choose to deal with clients with a certain net worth. There is nothing wrong with this as specialized help is needed by some and should be available. If the advisor that you are interviewing tells you that based on your funds available for investment, he can meet with you less than once a year or will call you instead of set a meeting, you may be able to infer that he is looking for a specific market and his services may not be right for you. You should expect a review at least once a year, regardless of your balance.

4. What current professional designations or standings do you hold?

As with any profession, it is important to stay on top of new developments and processes within your industry. The same goes for advisors and planners. Those who take the time and money to invest in their education, invest in you, helping your money work harder for you. Those advisors who carry such designations as CFP® (Certified

Financial Planner), or CGA (Certified General Accountant) have taken considerable steps to better understand the financial markets and how they apply to retirement and estate planning as well as dealing with tax treatment of investments. Individuals with these and a variety of other degrees take pride in doing what they do.

5. Are you a full service planner?

A full service financial provider or advisor will have access to stocks, mutual funds, and insurance products and solutions. It is NOT necessary for you to have a full service provider, unless you have specific goals and needs to be addressed, but it is helpful if the planner has colleagues available to provide these services if he/she cannot. Many firms offer full service through various branches of their operations. An advantage to having a full service advisor is that they can look at your overall financial situation and have the working knowledge of the different avenues available to solve different financial problems.

6. How do you get paid?

There are several ways that financial advisors get paid. Some advisors work strictly on commis-

sion from products and funds sold, while others work on a "fee for service" basis taking a percentage of the assets held or charging a flat fee each year. Still other advisors use a combination of the two methods. Make sure that the advisor you choose is honest and transparent about how they generate their income.

The truth about advisors is that unless you are licensed to buy and sell stocks and/or mutual funds, you will need to find a firm or dealer to do this for you. Remember that you are providing the advisor with business and therefore you should come first. If you don't like what you see or hear, or feel that your questions are not answered clearly and directly, find someone who will listen to what you need, and act appropriately.

This is a relationship-based business and if you feel the potential advisor would not be able to build a relationship with you and your family then they are not for you.

CHAPTER 6

Insurance Facts You Need To Know

Regardless of how you feel about insurance, there are some facts you need to know when building your successful financial plan. It amazes us how individuals pay for auto and home insurance without question yet balk at the idea of purchasing insurance to protect their families in the event of death, disability, or critical illness. Granted, if you pass away, you won't be thinking much about what you have left behind, but those who are left with your mortgage and debts will be thinking about it—ALOT!

Life Insurance

If someone told you that you could provide your family with income and funds to eliminate all your debt upon your death for less than the price of a cup of coffee per day wouldn't you look into it?

Surprisingly many people say NO!

Plan A	Plan B
No Life Insurance	Own life insurance leaving family financially secure

Look at the two above plans. Seems simple enough you may say. We have a question for you.

"If this were the day after you died, which plan would your family prefer?" Plan A or Plan B?

If you chose plan B which you most likely will,

then why would you not do something about it today while you are still healthy enough to qualify at a lower rate/cost, rather than waiting until you become ill and potentially be unable to qualify?

In today's consumer focused society, life insurance is more important than ever. Whether you choose a low cost term policy or invest in a permanent form of insurance, taking care of your obligations should be forefront in your mind when building your dreams and meeting with an advisor. Let's go over the difference between term insurance and permanent insurance contracts.

Term

This form of insurance is most commonly used by individuals or families that want to provide the needed lump sum of cash to their families should they pass away prematurely. The cost per thousand is less and the rates decrease at certain amounts such as $250,000 or $500,000. The funds provided by term insurance (and all life insurance) are paid tax free to the named beneficiary upon claim. There are many types available with common names such as term 10, 20 year term, term to age 100, or joint term policies which pay out on the first or last death of those insured under the policy. The most common Term 10 policy has a fixed premium amount (what you pay per month or per year) for 10 years and the contract then renews for another 10 years at a higher fixed rate. The increase in premium after 10 years is made based on a higher age and risk after the first ten year period.

In order to apply for this insurance you need to speak with your financial or insurance professional. Based on your age, medical history, and the amount of insurance applied for, you may have to complete medical testing. This may include a blood test, paramedical, and/or urine collection. Before you skip past the rest of this chapter upon reading that, remember that you only need to do these tests once if you are in good health. Once the contract is issued and you have been approved, the insurance company cannot change it or request further medical information. Also, if you purchased term insurance and 2 years later were diagnosed with cancer, your contract still does not change. It would be difficult to apply for another policy after that diagnosis without incurring a rating or all out rejection.

Essentially when you purchase term insurance you are "renting" the insurance and the coverage will usually expire by age 65 or 85 and even age 100 if purchasing a term to 100 policy. Most families choose this type in the early years (age 20-40) because the cost is low while the benefit amount available is still substantial enough to cover any costs you may want to provide for. See the end of this chapter for a list of costs and provisions that life insurance can be used for.

The beauty of purchasing a term policy is that in the event you should become ill after purchasing the plan and be ineligible to purchase more insurance, most plans can be converted to permanent insurance that covers you for life at a fixed cost.

PERMANENT
(sometimes referred to as participating)

There are many forms of permanent insurance, and the name really indicates the difference between its term insurance counterpart. Permanent insurance means that the insurance contract is permanent once issued and accepted. As long as the premiums are paid on time, the insurance stays in force in almost all cases to age 100, at which time the full benefit amount is paid out to the owner, should you still be living. The cost is usually higher than term coverage, but the benefits to this insurance can outweigh the higher price in premium.

There are numerous reasons why one would buy permanent insurance and if affordable to the individual over the long term, this is the preferred option. Most permanent policies build a cash value that can be accessed via a policy loan or withdrawal of dividends that are paid to the policy as the years go by. In fact permanent insurance is a great way to establish a savings plan for a new child and provide them with coverage and cash when they become an adult and begin a life of their own.

The common types of permanent insurance include whole life, 20 pay life, limited pay to age 65, joint first or last to die policies, and universal life. All of these policy types pretty much tell you how long your obligation to pay the premiums for the coverage with their given names. "Whole life" you pay for your whole life with some exceptions, "20 pay" your premiums are payable for 20 years and so on. The exception to this is universal life policies that have many options for payment and investment options linked to the policy.

Starting to get confused? To find out if a universal life policy is best for you, speak with your financial or insurance professional.

Typically, the cash values of these plans are lower in the first 15 years but grow substantially after that due to compounding of the dividends and building value in the plan.

Most people will require some form of life insurance coverage at every stage in life and it is recommended that the earlier you apply the more cost effective the plan will be. There is a high cost of waiting.

Age & Cost difference	Annual Premium
Male age 25 non-smoker, $100,000 whole life insurance	$1,573 per year Approx. cost
Male age 55 non-smoker, $100,000 whole life insurance	$4,321 per year Approx. cost

In the example, the male age 25 pays $78,650 until death/termination at age 75, or $7,770 less than the male age 55 and he got 30 more years of coverage. Male age 55 pays out $86,420 until death/termination of policy at age 75.

If your funds are limited, consider some permanent coverage and have a term rider attached to make up the shortfall to cover the mortgage and dependant income needed. Over time as your mortgage is paid down and your available savings funds go up, convert part of the term to permanent to begin building savings that can be used in the later years close to retirement or beyond.

Bank vs. Personally Owned Insurance

When you go to your bank to finance the purchase of your house, you are typically asked or required to have life insurance in place. The bank offers plans (typically group term plans) that cover the mortgage amount and the benefits are paid to the bank upon your passing. But BUYER BEWARE—these policies are usually not underwritten until the time of death. This means that no medical testing is done or records accessed to determine eligibility of the claim until you have passed away. If it is determined that you were not eligible for the insurance at the time of writing, no benefit is paid out under the contract. Only the premiums paid for the life of the policy are refunded. While this does not happen often, it DOES happen. Why would anyone want to take that chance?

As mentioned above, the benefits that could potentially be paid out are paid directly to your lender, not to your loved ones. With a personally owned policy you name the beneficiary(ies), and the proceeds are paid directly to them. Bank policies can also be decreasing term which reduces the amount of benefit as the mortgage principal decreases. That means that just because you purchased a $250,000 bank term policy, the amount payable upon your death may only be $200,000 depending on your outstanding mortgage balance. The other $50,000 is lost.

Consider this. You make the choice to purchase an individual policy vs. bank offered insurance and your partner passes away. The whole death benefit (amount of coverage) is paid out from the policy. Let's use $250,000 as an example. Rather than the bank paying only the balance of the mortgage, you could make the decision of keeping the funds, investing them in a conservative investment that pays a modest return of 5%. You would then have $12,500 in interest each year to help pay the mortgage payments and at the end of the day you still have $250,000 and are paying off the mortgage balance with the interest. Keep in mind this only works depending on interest rates at the time of death, so speaking with your advisor would be wise; and considering that you just lost your loved one and may not be thinking clearly, seeing your advisor is the best choice. So really, buying individual coverage may also be more cost effective and gives you complete control over the cash!

We urge you to make your own informed decision about life insurance, and seek out information that relates directly to your situation. Don't leave your family with unnecessary burdens at what would be a devastating time in their lives.

Disability Insurance

Disability insurance contracts are wide and varied with some employers offering coverage as part of a benefits package, some inexpensive that don't require medical evidence or underwriting until the time of claim, and non-cancelable policies that once issued and accepted are permanent and cannot be changed regardless of potential changes to insurability in the future.

If you are the main breadwinner in the family, it's important that you look at this coverage, as 1 in 3 Canadians can expect to suffer from a disability that prevents them from returning to work for 6 months or longer. We could inundate you with many facts and figures about age classes and the expected disability rate within each class, but it all boils down to the same message as life insurance, if you become disabled and can't work, who is going to pick up the monthly grocery and mortgage costs? Your friends or family? Your RRSP? Savings? How long would that last?

Depending on your occupation, income earned, and medical history, rates per month for this coverage vary widely.

Medical underwriting similar to life insurance underwriting is done at the time of application and in more cases than life insurance, ratings or exclusions are made as part of the contract. Most people facing a rating or exclusion on these contracts get upset and discard the policy as a whole. This is so foolish!

Imagine that you are a carpenter, you have had a back injury in the past but have not needed treatment for over 2 years. You apply for a policy and it comes back with an exclusion for any and all future back injuries. At first glance, you say "Why do I want to pay out good money for this when my back which could stand to get injured again is excluded?"

Yes, it's true that under the contract you cannot make claim for future back injuries, but what if you put a nail through your hand, or fall off a building and break your legs or suffer a brain injury, stroke or heart attack? The exclusion would only be on your back, so if you took the modified policy, all those other injuries would be covered. Would you really discard coverage for one or two exclusions when over 100+ other injuries are covered?

The benefit of owning personal disability policies has expanded considerably in the past few years. Additions and add ons to policies make the choice to look into this coverage a good one. Such additions include return of premium which pays you a percentage of total premiums paid at a specific anniversary (ex. age 55) should you not use the policy to pay benefits. This return can be anywhere from 50% to 70% depending on the insurance carrier. Another option that business owners should look at is partial disability and future income protection. Partial disability will pay a percentage of benefits should you be able to perform only a limited percentage of your regular job load. A future income protection option provides the option to purchase additional monthly benefit amounts as your income grows (usually $200-$1,500) at specified times throughout the life of the policy. Financial evidence is required to support the additions at the time of addition to the policy.

Disability insurance contracts typically run to age 65 and do not build a cash value. If you are the main income earner in your household, or your income is needed to provide for monthly expenses, speak with your insurance provider today about how disability insurance can help safeguard you against potential loss upon injury or illness preventing you from working. So many families wipe out savings and get deep into debt as a result of injury when the solution has been available for a relatively modest premium for many years.

A final note on disability coverage that you purchase and pay for: the benefits provided under the policy are tax free. If you claim for benefits of $2,500 per month and the claim is accepted, the $2,500 is paid tax free! That reduces the burden on your finances even more.

Do understand though that if your disability coverage is provided through your group benefits at work and your employer pays any part of the premium, the benefit collected would be taxable.

Critical Illness Insurance

We are very excited about this valuable and relatively new kind of coverage available to people in North America. Critical illness insurance policies are policies that can be personally owned and applied for or are sometimes part of a group benefits package.

Essentially critical illness insurance provides the owner and insured with a lump sum of tax free cash, upon diagnosis of a critical illness or disease and survival of that particular illness past 30 days. Under a basic contract the following is covered:

- Life Threatening Cancer

- Stroke

- Heart Attack

As with other insurance products, the coverage applied for is medically underwritten at the time of application and evidence (blood test, vitals) is required with the application. The lump sum of cash the insurance provides can be used to pay the costs of treatment, pay for monthly living expenses, take a holiday, or anything that you desire or require in the event of suffering from such an injury or disease.

As the market broadens there are various types of coverage available, some in the form of term type coverage which sets a fixed premium for coverage and increases the premium after 10 years or a permanent kind which sets a lifetime price to age 65 or 75 typically. Options to add onto the basic policy include enhanced coverage which covers the diagnosis of diseases and injuries such as Parkinson disease, blindness, bypass surgery or other. The return of premium option can also be applied to this policy as with disability coverage.

Again, beware of the bank's coverage! Banks are offering disability and critical illness coverage when lending for mortgages or other loans, but remember—the insurance may not be medically underwritten until the time of claim. Just like life insurance coverage from the banks, if you purchased their critical illness coverage, suffered a covered illness and at the time of claim discovered that you never qualified for the coverage, nothing is paid out to you except the premiums you have paid. Have your advisor discuss the options you have been presented with.

What can insurance pay for?

- mortgage costs
- loan balances
- education plans
- groceries
- time away from work
- utility bills
- savings plans
- funeral costs
- charitable benefits
- gifts to your church or organization
- capital gains on property transferred to your heirs
- taxes payable upon your death

The list is truly endless.

CHAPTER 7

Investments: How much should I be saving, and what should I invest in?

There have been many well known publications that have gone on exhaustively about exactly how much we should be putting away for retirement and future goals. Of course, because everyone's situation is individual, your strategy for saving should be tailored specifically for you.

Advisors and planners have access to outstanding software that can project for you just how much you will need to start saving today to purchase that shiny new car in 3 years, or the condo you liked so much to relax in. Also, advisors can calculate for you how your savings for future income will grow over time and with compound interest, capital gains, and dividends.

As we stated earlier, everyone's situation is individual, however a good rule of thumb for most individuals and families is to invest 10% of your gross monthly earnings (income pre taxes and deductions) to a retirement plan. As will be explained later in this chapter, there are a multitude of ways to put this money to work and get options that align closely with your needs.

If your employer offers you a group RRSP that matches contributions as you make them, TAKE FULL ADVANTAGE OF THIS PLAN. Nowhere else will you receive up to a 100% instant return on your money with no risk!

If you are currently reading this and looking at lowering debt obligations for the near term, then it is probably prudent to start small contributions. A monthly contribution of even $50 to a retirement savings plan grows over time and as your debt is lowered, you can increase contributions to come into line with the 10% paying yourself first idea or more if you have had a late start.

Understanding the Basics

In today's marketplace there are so many investment names, numbers, companies and dealers that it is understandably hard to decipher what each actually is and what it does and represents. Have you found yourself looking at all the mail you get and feel unable to read or comprehend the information you've been sent about your money? Regarding investments, there are two main types available for purchase. Of course there are many more options and allocations within but these are beyond the scope of this section.

First and most conservative

Fixed Income: These are funds/stocks that invest primarily in GICs, T-Bills, and Bonds and provide a steady income with little to no risk. That being said, these funds also provide a lower rate of return on capital and little chance of large growth for both the short and long term.

Second and NOT conservative

Equity Investments (added risk with potential added returns).

Canadian Equity: These are funds/stocks that invest in a wide variety of companies, within Canada. These can be new companies, ones that are experiencing growth and companies that are on the decline. These funds typically fluctuate much more in value and price than fixed income products, but the potential for growth and in some investments, tax preferred earnings are much higher in contrast to fixed income funds.

A second type of equity investment with further added risk is:

Global Equity: These funds/stocks invest again in a wide variety of companies, governments etc OUTSIDE of Canada. Some are specific to a region or country and their value is dependant on how that particular economy is doing or the events taking place that could potentially affect the funds. As well, these funds typically fluctuate more than a fixed income product, but can potentially offer higher returns and preferred tax treatment on the profits or returns. Further risk is added in foreign currency investments, as now you are dealing with currency changes as well as buying into foreign companies.

We could literally write a whole book on the two classes of investments and other financial products available for purchase but what we have provided is a snapshot of how they operate and fit (or don't) into your financial and investment planning.

For those folks closer to retirement, and looking at a fixed income for their future, the goal in most cases is to put a large portion of the investable funds into a fixed income fund or mix of. This allows the retiree to preserve their capital (i.e. keep the initial amount invested) and still earn modest interest on their account while drawing from it in future years. Depleting capital or not becomes a personal choice depending on one's feelings toward estate planning.

For families and individuals in their 20s-mid

40s, the plan is usually to keep adding funds to a savings plan with the idea that they will not be drawing funds from this plan until they reach their retirement goal in the future.

Most in this category want a mix of equity funds and fixed incomes because the earnings which are typically higher in equity funds can potentially be taxed at a preferred rate and with the time horizon usually over 15-20 years, most can accept some market fluctuation as it evens out throughout the savings years.

For families and individuals in their 50s – 60s, the focus is primarily on when and how to exit the working stage. While the trend seems to be that individuals are working well into their 60s and beyond, because retirement options may not be available or they are simply bored at home, the focus should still be on retaining the growth and capital that has been attained over the earning years. If proper planning and saving has been done, then starting to spend the capital earned should begin at this stage.

THINKING LONG TERM
AT EVERY STAGE

No matter what stage of life you are in, you need to think for the long term when it comes to investing.

If you are young, your long term view is going to be much longer than an elder, however depending on your current financial situation will dictate what you invest for the very long term and what you need to keep available for the short term.

What we know from historical reporting is that everything goes in cycles. What we don't know is how long each cycle will last.

Two reasons why people invest that are important for you to consider are:

GREED, and

FEAR

When we get greedy and try to take more from what is logically and legally possible we end up typically getting slapped hard. It's easy to get caught up with the crowd that is bragging and saying "You HAVE to invest in this, we've been raking in 25% returns and everything is wonderful!"

Let's be realistic when we plan, the 25% will not last. Eventually that investment that has been making these extraordinary returns will collapse or even disappear. Recall the tech boom of the 90s that came to a crashing halt, or the most recent US insurance and financial company crashes. The technology didn't crash, fear in the markets and investors made this happen.

Not to say that there is not a chance that you can recover your losses, but this will take time and patience. This is where "fear" comes in.

Investors get worried about the investments they choose (or had chosen for them) and spend sleepless nights thinking about it. The fear eats these people up and so they sell.

Sadly, once they have sold, they ended up doing exactly what they feared the most: "They bought high and sold low."

Don't make investment decisions that you can't live with and don't invest from a greed or fear perspective. Invest on logic and the fundamentals of the investment that will help you achieve both your long and short term goals.

CHAPTER 8

TAXES

Here is your biggest expense in life and it should not be ignored.

Where do we start with this one....

We would first advise that in most cases if you hire a good accountant or tax preparer, they will no doubt save you much more in taxes then they will ever cost you!!

That's not to say we should all run out today to find an accountant. If you are the mom & pop type basic tax return with one or two T4's in the family with some investments, you could go it alone. However at this level it's even good to get an opinion from someone who is up to date on tax rates and new developments that could affect you.

If you have more holdings (investments), a company, a proprietorship, or a partnership, you should no doubt seek out a good tax professional to assist you with tax planning going forward. There are so many changes to the government tax system each year that a tax planner can apply to your personal situation.

Now you can see why tax planning plays an important if not crucial role in your financial plan.

This chapter is not designed to educate you on taxes (that's far too complex an issue), it's in-tent is to bring awareness to the importance of tax planning. This is true especially when one becomes successful with one's finances.

Without getting complex, let's relate our tax lesson to your investments.

As mentioned in the previous chapter, you have Fixed Income Investments. Fixed income provides exactly that—income. Therefore it is taxed as if it was earned income from your regular employment. It is also taxed at your marginal tax rate based on your income level.

What's your marginal tax rate?

Shown in the chart on the following page is what our government uses as our tax system. It is known as a graduating system and as you can see by the chart, the more income you make, the higher rate of tax you are going to pay. This is your marginal tax rate.

2007 Marginal Tax Rates in Percentages

Tax Bracket	Regular Income	Capital Gains	Regular Dividends
0-$8,929	0	0	0
$8,930-$9,027	15.55	7.78	2.71
$9,028-$34,396	21.55	10.78	3.90
$34,397-$37,177	24.65	12.33	7.78
$34,178-$68,793	31.15	15.58	15.90
$68,794-$74,356	33.70	16.85	19.09
$74,357-$78,983	37.70	18.85	24.09
$78,984-$95,908	39.70	19.85	26.59
$95,909-$120,887	40.70	20.35	27.84
$120,888+	43.70	21.85	31.59

Find current rates at aaronvissia.com

As an example say you are earning $50,000 per year. Your marginal tax rate is 31.15% today. These rates tend to change on an annual basis but not always. The bottom line here is that if you earn money (interest) from fixed income investments, you will give 31% to the government.

If you invest in equities, your earnings have the potential to earn capital gains and dividends. Looking back at the tax chart, you will see that capital gains and dividends are tax preferred type earnings subject to a lower rate of taxation.

Be warned that you may not want to put all your money in equities just to save tax. The equities can come at a much higher risk. Their value will fluctuate and if you need the money when the equities are low, you may lose.

Again, the key is to find the balance between fixed income and equity investments that match your risk tolerance and your tax strategy.

Finally, we need to mention again that there are many rules and regulations in place regarding your investment options as they relate to taxation. Unless you spend much more time researching taxes and the associated strategies, find the right professional to assist you with this area of planning.

CHAPTER 9

PUTTING ALL YOUR EGGS IN ONE BASKET - The Common Myth

This chapter may be one of the most important within these pages. I have heard so many times from clients that they do not want to invest all of their savings with one planner/advisor or institution for fear of "losing the whole basket".

Please let me clarify exactly what the statement means concerning savings and investments.

If you had $100,000 to invest and these were all of the funds you owned, you have several choices for investing with someone or an institution.

Scenario 1. You want to make sure that you don't lose at least half of it so you deposit $50,000 into a 3 year GIC earning approx. 2.75% interest. You would like to see growth on your original amount and you have heard that a local company has been doing great things with some clients. You meet with this company and deposit $25,000 with them into an equity fund which the company assures you will earn at least 10% in the year to come. You don't know a lot about it but if other people say the company is good, they must be right.

Finally, you get a call from your local advisor to meet to discuss your policies. When you meet he tells you that he offers a specialty fund which will outperform the market because of the increase in oil and gas stocks and you would be sorry to miss out on this opportunity.

You deposit $15,000 with the advisor and keep $10,000 in the bank "in case".

Fast forward a year.

The statements have come in and here is how it looks:

GIC Value $50,458.33
Equity Fund $26,000.00 (earned 4%)
Specialty Fund $12,300.00 (lost 18%)
Bank $10,000

Total: $98,758.33

Scenario 2: Knowing that these funds need to grow for your retirement, and realizing that you do not have enough sophisticated knowledge of various funds and investments, you contact your local advisor. She meets with you and does a fact find to figure out exactly what your plans and goals are, how much risk you can tolerate, and where your overall comfort level lies. After the initial meeting, the advisor comes back to you with a plan. She brings illustrations and information and lays out the following strategy:

As the majority of these funds will become income in later years, she recommends that you deposit $70,000 into a fund account that allocates the funds based on your own tolerance level. This happens to be "conservative". She explains that while you should not expect huge returns on these funds in the next 5-10 years, you can be confident that they will earn approx. 5% a year. At that point you stop her and say, "I don't want to have all that money tied up in one place if the markets go down, I don't know if I am comfortable with this". The advisor smiles and indicates that she understands. She isn't placing all your funds into one place, rather she is placing proportionate amounts of the total within several funds to diversify the risk and ensure that should one market go up and another down, your interests will average out.

The advisor is also concerned with your liquidity and possible need for some of these funds should an emergency arise. She recommends taking $20,000 and placing the funds into a money market account to gain modest growth, eliminate any possibility of fees upon transfer out and ensure that they are readily available should you need them. At the end of one year, if you have not had a need for the money in this account, you can transfer a portion of the money into the growth plan mentioned above.

Finally, the advisor talks about growth funds. She explains that because you are considered a conservative advisor and should not be primarily invested in growth or equity type funds, but do want to see an increase on the initial capital, you should place a small portion of the funds into a proven growth investment. She has done some research for you and put together a list of 4 proven funds with a leading mutual fund company. She explains each one to you, the past returns, the holdings and sector weightings. You see one that is of particular interest to you and suggest using that fund. The advisor agrees and it is decided that you will put the final $10,000 in that plan.

Again, a year goes by and the statements are in:

Allocation Fund Plan: $73,500.00 (earned 5%)
Money Market Plan: $20,350.00 (earned 1.75%)
Growth Fund: $ 10,650.00 (earned 6.5%)

Total: $104,500.00

Obviously, the investments in scenario 2 did better than those in scenario 1. Most individuals assume that putting your eggs in one basket means dealing with one advisor to handle all your savings and retirement plan needs. But that is not what the phrase actually means.

As illustrated (and this is just an example) in scenario 1, the client did not want to give all their funds to one advisor or bank to handle. They wanted to spread the funds around assuming that this would better diversify them. In the end, they lost not only in terms of returns of the funds, but also because no single advisor knew their whole situation and so could not make a plan that would provide for all their needs and risk tolerance to various funds.

Again, we will emphasize the importance of finding the right advisor to assist you with diversifying your investment portfolio. Make sure that in your initial meeting, they are asking more questions about you; this means they want to learn about you and how they can best advise you for your particular situation and goals!

Remember when investing that in addition to RRSP's, you can now invest in the Tax Free

Savings Account that allows those at the age of majority to contribute $5,000 per year without being taxed on the growth, and you can withdraw at any time. You don't lose your contribution room and unused amounts carry over to the next year. This is a great way to establish an emergency fund.

CHAPTER 10

Specialized Options for Investing

While the intention of this book is to help provide the basics about financial planning, debt reduction, and working within an achievable budget, it is important to briefly outline some of the other options that you have for achieving financial independence.

These options are not for everyone, and if you

are an individual or family working to become debt free, I don't recommend implementing any of these options until you have been working with a budget successfully for at least 2-3 years. As well, you will definitely want to seek professional advice when looking to diversify your savings and add income and growth from these avenues.

REAL ESTATE

Donald Trump has made and lost a fortune with it, many infomercials talk about how you can achieve financial freedom quickly with it, but how does it really work?

There are many routes that you can take to benefit from owning real estate outside of your primary residence, and really, you can customize a long term plan for yourself and/or your family with some research and discussion with a local realty professional. The main options are:

A. Rental Properties

B. Fix up and Flip properties

C. Commercial Rental Properties

D. Buy now & Hold for later Flip Properties

A. Rental Properties

As someone who has personally invested in rental income properties, we know first hand the background research and work that needs to be done when looking to invest in this sector of real estate. The concept is actually very simple. Purchase a property with one or multiple rental units which provides a monthly income that covers the mortgage, monthly water or hydro fees, taxes, and insurance PLUS provides you with a net income. Sounds easy? Think again.

In today's world of low interest rates (that can go up at any time), interest only mortgages, and increased amortization options, many people are delving into the rental income game. Before you sign your name to a title and become a landlord, you owe it to yourself to be diligent in looking at every angle first.

1. Canadian mortgages work differently than our US counterpart and it is important to understand that. If you want to purchase a property and get the best rate possible, in most cases you NEED to have at least 25%

of the selling price to use as a downpayment. TV infomercials often illustrate how people just like you became rich by purchasing properties with little to no money down. This option is only available to you if you have proven history with your bank or lender in completing successful real estate deals or if you live in the USA. Canadian Mortage Housing Corporation does have some options that reduce the downpayment but you will need to occupy one of the residences that you own in a given property and be using it as your primary residence. Also remember that you will pay a premium to use a lower down payment.

2. In the event that all of your units on a given property were vacant, could you carry the costs (mortgage payment, insurance, hydro, property taxes) yourself? If you don't have the disposable income in your budget to pay for those expenses, you don't want to sign the deal. Defaulting on any mortgage can and will jeopardize your credit rating and impact your ability to borrow in the future. What if your property needs a new roof in the near term? You should have the funds available

to make repairs and renovations if the need presents itself.

3. Location, location, location. It is important to spend at least 3-6 months looking at the particular market or township that you want to purchase in. Ask these questions:

- What is the outlook for the local economy? Are there new stores and opportunities for growth coming in?

- What does the local rental pool look like now? What are the costs to rent, what is the supply vs. demand in the area, and what is the average age of renters in the city?

- What are the prices like for the type of property you are looking for? What did they sell for in the last 3 years vs. now, and what are the projected property assessment values expected to be?

- Where in the city or town are you looking to purchase? Is the area considered a better or worse part of the city? Is there shopping and local bus routes close by?

4. What type of renters do you want to deal with? Working families, students, retirees, and low income individuals are just a few of the rental population worth investing in. You need to know what your expectations are in advance and this will help you decide whom you want to deal with on an ongoing basis. Problems always arise and unless you have property management in place, it's you that will have to deal with them.

5. Becoming a landlord or hiring a property management firm. Be realistic about the time you have available to take care of renters, vacancies and maintenance. This will cost you in time, especially if you have a vacancy that needs to be filled and some clean up work to do in the unit to have it ready to show. If you don't have the time needed to commit to these tasks, then you will want to consider having someone outside manage the property for you. But this comes at a cost as well. Management fees are approx. 10-18% of the gross monthly rents. Factor this cost in when looking at properties.

Once you have done some research, get the local papers, an up-to-date real estate guide for the area you are interested in, and have a look around. While a picture is worth a thousand words, seeing the property in person is worth everything. A good rule of thumb is to look at about 100 listings that fall into your desired property type before you make an offer on anything. Remember that rents paid to you are taxable as earned income, however you can deduct expenses from this income.

When you meet with a real estate professional to have a look at specific properties, bring your camera, a note pad, and put your thinking cap on. Be on the lookout for old and faulty electrical, plumbing, and foundations. Pay attention to the state of the property with the current renters in place. Ask how long they have been living in the residence and how long they plan to stay.

A good realtor will explain to you the potential for the property and go over the current cash flow and what you can expect in the future. Work closely with them so that they understand exactly what you want and can get it for you. Many good properties sell prior to becoming listed, so ensure that you are on a buyers list with a reputable professional. Don't let a potential cash cow pass you by.

B. Fix Up and Flip Properties

This type of real estate investment is fairly self-explanatory. Find a property that is selling below the market value, fix it up, and sell it for a profit. As applies to rental income properties, unless you plan to live in the residence while completing the renovations, you need at least 25% down to get a good mortgage rate.

Ask yourself if you have the time and funds available to make the necessary repairs and additions. As mentioned above, be realistic about the costs you will incur vs. the potential payoff. Many people have done well by fixing and flipping, but this success usually occurs after several years of experience and the ability to complete the work yourself in a timely manner.

Use the same guidelines in doing your research as listed previously to ensure the decision is right for you. Also, don't forget that the "flip" triggers capital gains tax if you do not live in the residence that you fix up.

C. Commercial Rental Properties

Imagine owning a building that houses a successful dentist and doctor's practice, a new restaurant and several long term businesses. The potential for rental and lease income can be staggering.

Commercial real estate is again treated differently for lending purposes than residential real estate. Amortization schedules, interest rates, and repayment terms can vary depending on the actual situation.

Most investors in this sector have tenants on longer term leases with specific conditions and clauses that need to be determined in advance. A word to get used to if looking to enter this market is "leasehold improvements". If you purchase a shell building without current tenants, you may choose to build the offices and spaces yourself thus being able to charge a higher lease rate, or you can leave it to the tenant to finish their space at a reduced lease rate. Again, it all comes down to time, cost, and the ability to self manage or not. Your real estate professional can direct you towards those properties that best suit your needs and desires.

D. Buy Now & Hold to Flip Later

The concept of purchasing a real estate property with the idea of flipping it in the future for a profit is not new. This type of investment is more for individuals who have solid financial plans in place and can afford to pay the mortgage until the market turns to their favor and they can sell.

Just as with purchasing rental income properties, serious research needs to be done prior to committing to a purchase and you definitely need to speak with your financial advisor and real estate professional before you take on a venture like this. You will also need to consult with an accountant to see how such a purchase impacts your bottom line for tax planning purposes.

It's tricky to anticipate the ups and downs of the real estate market but there are huge potential profits to be made if you are a smart investor who gives careful consideration to all the pros and cons of entering into this type of investment.

INTELLECTUAL INVESTMENTS

The name sounds complicated but actually the concept is fairly easy to understand. You may be using this investment strategy already and not even know it!

Essentially using your intellect as an investment can mean being an entrepreneur, artist, writer, or business owner. Anytime that you leverage your ability to create something, or provide a service to earn a profit for yourself, you are making an intellectual investment. Many of us have good ideas about products, services or ideas that could benefit a large or specific group of people, but we shy away from implementing anything based on a fear of something. Rather than taking what can be a calculated risk with proper research, people stay where they are and don't broaden their horizons to make use of talents and abilities that they possess.

If you have an idea or concept that you feel would be of benefit to all or a part of a group of people, push yourself out of your comfort zone and explore the possibilities of implementing the idea. We have all heard the phrase "You never know unless you try," and we really feel that more individuals and families could experience more satisfaction and financial freedom by following their hearts and using the talents that they were blessed with. The people that have developed products you see on your shopping channel all started from scratch and had the courage to see the idea through to success.

That all being said we have a big caution before deciding to start a business or developing a product or service. It's true that many businesses that start up fail within one year. While the factors in this happening are wide and varied, a common thread is often that inadequate planning was done. If you need to have a large sum of money ready to develop your idea, speak with your financial advisor about how to properly prepare yourself. You don't want to get halfway through the process and be unable to complete it due to bad financial planning and a lack of necessary funds.

As with all investments, do your research and talk about the idea with your family, friends, and peers that you trust. Your key to enjoying financial independence may be waiting for you inside your own head!!

STOCKS & LEVERAGING

We will speak only in general terms about investing in the stock market and derivatives (often referred to as options).

When interest rates are low, borrowing money and investing to earn a profit seems to be the "in" thing to do. Some individuals and families are even taking funds from built up equity in their homes to dabble in the markets. We strongly caution the "average" family about making a move like this because the markets can and do change and what looked like a promising return can quickly change into debt that takes years to repay.

Essentially, the stock market is a general term used to refer to the organized trading of securities through various exchanges and through the over-the-counter market. A "stock exchange" is a specific form of a stock market, a physical location where stocks and bonds are bought and sold, such as the New York Stock Exchange, or Toronto Stock Exchange (TSX). These stocks and bonds on a particular market are issued by companies, corporations, governments and other related organizations.

Again, if you are well on your way to saving to provide for your future goals and plans for yourself and/or your family and you have your consumer spending under control, you may have a chunk of disposable funds to "play" in the markets with. There are various ways to get into the markets, using a stock broker, an online investor service, or going through a financial institution that provides this service. Regardless of how you choose to get into this market, the ball falls squarely in your lap should something happen with your money. I strongly recommend that you do much research about where you want to invest, your time horizon and expectations, as well as the losses you are willing to accept. You have NO control over the stock market.

Purchasing and trading stocks is not free, so be wary of becoming a day trader if you are not fully versed in how your broker or brokerage works. But as with all investments both simple and complex, the potential to gain is there, just make sure you've done your homework and a lot of it on the particular company you are buying! If you deal with a broker make sure he/she does their homework as well.

COMMODITIES

By far one of the best specialized investment areas to get into modestly, commodities purchases are something to consider for your financial future. This is not to be confused with buying and selling gold or silver stocks, but rather, purchasing actual gold and silver bars, coins, or ingots.

If you have disposable income, consider using 20% for the ongoing purchase of gold and silver. Speculators have been preaching that the price of gold per ounce is expected to hit over $1,000 USD before the 2008 year is done. Silver bars have been on the rise with the price a mere $11 USD per ounce in the first quarter 2007, and prices close to $20 USD.

This is a great way to save money and build growth for the long term. You can start small and purchase 1-10gram pieces or coins with ¼ ounces of gold, or purchase silver 1 ounce coins in quantities of 5 or more.

To purchase gold or silver you need to do some homework and pay attention to the spot price of gold around the time you wish to purchase.

Find a reputable gold bullion dealer in your town (these can be coin dealers, banks, or currency dealers) and meet with him to enquire about how often he gets these products in. Typically dealers are quite honest and only charge a small percentage on top of the fixed price for the day of purchase. Developing a relationship with a dealer will ensure that you are called when new shipments come in.

You can also buy gold and silver on line with well known commodities dealers, however these dealers usually have minimums in place that are quite high. Ebay is also a place to purchase—as long as you know the price per ounce when you are purchasing. Pay attention to shipping costs on this site as well, it could inflate the price dramatically.

Buying gold and silver is a great investment for children or grandchildren and of course for retirement or estate purposes.

COINS

When purchasing gold or silver coins for the gold value alone, beware of those coins that have a value based on a key date coin or specialty coin. If you want to purchase these types of coins as a hobby, that's fine, but for investment purposes buy it for the gold content only.

I know of a gentlemen who 30 years ago made a point of purchasing one ounce of gold every two weeks when he received his pay cheque. His goal was to redeem one bar every month in retirement to offset some of his expenses. HE DID IT!! Considering that the price of gold per ounce 30 years ago was around $170 USD with an incredible bottoming out to $105 in 1976. Yes, the price can rise and fall dramatically, overall the rate of return for the long term is good.

Consult your financial planner about how commodities can fit into your financial plan. It's not for everyone, but the majority of individuals and families that are putting funds away for the future could stand to invest in this sector.

Finally after you have made the decision to purchase gold or silver, make an investment in a safety deposit box if you don't currently have one. No one wants to lose these valuable pieces and once you start to accumulate them, it's just not smart to keep them at home.

CHAPTER 11

Financial Success & Failure

Both of us have been fortunate to have entered
the financial industry as a career in these times
of extraordinary opportunity and potential failure. As such, we have been able to help people
on both sides of the fence.

We see individuals who are very financially successful by virtue of their own efforts and we've seen the decisions they make that got them to where they are today.

On the flipside, we have met with people who have experienced financial failure. Sadly, a trend seems to follow those who choose to fail or succeed.

Financial failure is the easiest route and usually comes with the desire to want something today without sacrifice or doing the work (earning income) to get it.

The difference between success and failure is self-discipline and making the right choices for the long term, not being short sighted and thinking only for what you want today.

Now we are not saying that successful people don't make mistakes along the way. They do, but with an important difference. Financially successful people learn from their mistakes and never repeat them.

People who fail continuously repeat their bad decisions and often feel like they are never given a fair shake or their "share" of financial success. This "poor me" attitude sets a standard for a constant pattern that often flows into other areas of these individual's lives.

LEARNING FROM OUR ELDERS

Have you ever sat with an elder and asked them about their take on money and finance? You should.

For the most part we see the elder generation as stewards of a mass of capital. Eventually they will be passing these funds on to the next generation, but how did they build all this wealth in the first place?

For the most part, they will tell you that they worked hard, and they did. They will also tell you that they never bought something that they did not have the cash in hand for.

They scrimped and saved through investments usually of a fixed income type and when they had enough money to purchase the item that they desired or needed, they went ahead and made the purchase, getting a better deal even back then, because they paid with cash.

Today we have more wants and no thought is given to waiting for what we want. We want it all now and we want to be like the Jones.

Today we pay interest to have these "things", while our elders made interest while saving for the "things".

Who is and was wiser?

The times have not changed so much that what our parents and grandparents taught us about money has no merit. If you get the chance to sit and chat with an elder in your life ask them about money, we can all learn from some of the proven methods and strategies from the past.

Practice for success and take lessons and advice from those who know what they are talking about, based on solid experience.

CHAPTER 12

Putting It All Together

We've discussed how to realistically go over your current financial situation, make changes to reduce debt, and stick to a budget, put plans into place to safeguard you and your family against death and disability, choosing the right financial advisor to begin investing and saving for future goals, and looked at secondary investment strategies that can be used to boost your financial picture and provide sources of income and profit outside of employment income. What is left to ensure that your head is out of the sand and you are looking at your world and the world around you through a real and attainable lens?

One of the biggest challenges that our family "The Jones'" experienced was a lack of honest communication and quality time spent sharing and experiencing life's little moments together. Society is pushing us to become more fast paced and do more with less time. Before you rush off to make new plans and begin a sprint to finish first in your financial race, STOP!

TIME

If you were given a chance to look ahead in your life, say 10 years into the future, what would you like to see that would make you feel successful? After you answer that, see yourself as that person and head towards it.

"Appreciate the moments you have now, as the life clock picks up speed as you get older, time goes fast."

We hear it over and over from our elders. It's been told to us since we were very young. We tend to ignore that statement as a young child, always wanting to be a bit older. When we reach adulthood we start to realize that the statement is so very true. Time does fly by.

So what should we do about this?

We need to make the best of every minute, every hour, every day, and every year. Time truly is your most valuable asset and you can have control over it.

Be Productive!!

Being productive can mean many things. Working hard, thinking hard, planning, playing, talking, socializing, doing things for others, and relaxing can all be productive. Once today has ended, it will never be again, and you never get the chance to take back a day wasted.

Understand YOUR time and leverage it well. Everyone knows someone who has been diagnosed with a terminal illness or disease and if you asked them what if anything they would like to have, they will surely tell you: "more time."

Real life satisfaction and fulfillment comes from knowing what's really important to you and those in your life and making the time to do those little things that often get neglected.

Make sure that your life plan includes taking the time to listen to your spouse and children. Ask them about their dreams and goals and what's important to them.

Make time to do some of the labour around your house such as housecleaning, mowing the lawn, and planting a garden. Our grandparents and generations before them knew that the satisfaction that comes from a hard day's work spent at home was more valuable than making a good wage staying late at work. If people spent more time working with their hands and sweating a bit, I'm sure that better sleep and health would soon follow.

Spend time enjoying and cultivating the wondrous creation of nature around you. In today's day and age, we see more and more species and diverse ecosystems vanishing from the planet.

It has never been truer that what you see today may indeed be gone tomorrow. Do your part to keep our country and planet green and lush. Teach your children to respect the land and appreciate it in the same way. Keep in mind that it is the journey and not the destination that counts.

Lastly, LOVE. We can guarantee you that you have affected at least 200 people in your life and made them feel better or hurt them and made them feel worse, all through communication as serious as a personal conversation or as impersonal as an email. Think about what you say to people you meet at all life's stages, care for each one as you would want to be cared for yourself. It all boils down to the golden rule.

Do unto others as you'd have done to you!

ABOUT THE AUTHOR

Aaron Vissia, CFP Professional

Born and raised in Port Alberni, B.C., on Vancouver Island, Aaron has brought success and financial freedom to many individuals, families, and businesses in his various careers.

Starting as a young entrepreneur, Aaron had several business ventures that garnered him success and recognition within his community. Once he married and settled into domestic bliss, he decided to make a change. Joining the London Life organization in 1996, he began his career as a financial services provider.

Aaron's business has grown in leaps and bounds since its inception, having formed a corporation, Aaron Vissia Financial Inc, in 2004. Considered one of the best in B.C. amongst his peers, Aaron prides himself on utilizing his unique approach, My Plan©, to help people at all walks and stages of life reach financial success that is personalized to them. Aaron uses all of the strategies and suggestions in this book as part of his planning process with clients.

Aaron is well known as a community leader, serving as a director for the Alberni Valley Community Foundation and a regular contributor to Shaw TV community programming.

Father to Jessie and Jamie, Aaron is also kept busy with two growing girls and "all things sugar & spice". He and his wife of 14 years, Serena, enjoy spending time at the lake and traveling about exploring new places and meeting new people.

Aaron's strong belief in his community and the potential that lies within is what has made him successful in virtually every venture he has taken on. As he so modestly says, "the only limits on the future are those we place on ourselves".

Expenses Work Sheet

FINANCIAL
INCORPORATED

Lifestyle Expenses

Expenses	Monthly Amount	Expenses	Monthly Amount
Housing		**Other**	
☐ Home - Rent/Mortgage	_____	☐ Child Care	_____
☐ Natural Gas	_____	☐ Personal Care	_____
☐ Heating	_____	☐ Donations/Gifts	_____
☐ Electricity	_____	☐ General Household	_____
☐ Telephone	_____	☐ Education Costs/Savings	_____
☐ Cable/Internet Service	_____	☐ Non-Registered Savings	_____
☐ Municipal Taxes	_____	☐ Retirement Savings	_____
☐ Home Insurance	_____	☐ Medical/Dental	_____
☐ Maintenance	_____	☐ Life Insurance	_____
☐ Miscellaneous	_____	☐ Disability Insurance	_____
		☐ Miscellaneous	_____
Transportation			
☐ Automobile Payment	_____	**Loans**	
☐ Automobile Insurance	_____	☐ Personal	_____
☐ Gasoline	_____	☐ Student	_____
☐ Maintenance/Repairs	_____	☐ Business	_____
☐ Parking	_____	☐ Credit Card	_____
☐ Miscellaneous	_____		
Food and Entertainment			
☐ Groceries	_____		
☐ Restaurant	_____		
☐ Clubs/Memberships	_____		
☐ Recreation	_____		
☐ Miscellaneous	_____	Total Monthly Expenses _____	

$_____ - $_____ = $_____

Total Monthly Net Income *minus* **Total Monthly Expenses** *equals* **Disposable Income**

Sample Budget
for Debt Reduction

Bob and Rita have the following monthly expenses (after reductions to variable costs have been factored in).

Fixed Monthly Expenses

Mortgage- $850
Hydro (power only) - $80
Water- $35
Telephone- $55
Cable/Internet- $85
Home Insurance- $60
Property Taxes- $100
Car Insurance- $120
Gas- $320
Groceries- $650

Life Insurance- $120
Disability Insurance- $90
Donations- $100
Misc. (car repair/personal care) $125

Total this section: $2,790.00

Outstanding Consumer Debt

Mastercard balance: $5,689 (min pymt $100)

Car Loan: $14,900 (monthly pymt $329)

Big Box credit card balance: $1,420 (min pymt $50)

Line of Credit Balance: $3,100 (min pymt $85)

Short Term Goals

1. Have $1,000 for family wedding in 4 months.

2. Begin putting $25 per month away for RESP for children.

3. Save $600 for new hot water tank.

Income available and pay schedule

Bob: Bob is paid twice per month on the 15th and 30th of each month. His net paycheque is $1,425.00

Rita: Rita is paid per week and her net paycheque is $385.00

Using the above information, see what a sample budget for Bob and Rita looks like. We have assumed that the credit card accounts are closed and no further interest is charged, as well bank fees of approx. $10 are covered by the budget although not mentioned.

July

Rita: July 2, $385: $200 mortgage, $80 hydro, $100 groceries.

Rita: July 9, $385: $150 mortgage, $100 gas, $100 groceries, $35 water.

Bob: July 15, $1,425: $500 mortgage, $220 gas, $100 prop. Tax, $60 house ins, $210 life & disability insurance, $120 car insurance, $220 groceries.

Rita: July 16, $385: $85 cable, $140 groceries, $55 telephone, $100 donations.

Rita: July 23, $385: $100 groceries, $120 wedding, $165 MC.

Bob: July 30, $1,425: $330 car pymt, $400 LOC, $400 big box, $100 hot water tank, $125 miscell, $50 RESP.

Rita: July 30, $385: $200 big box, $100 wedding, $80 MC.

August

Rita: Aug 6, $385: $200 mortgage, $80 hydro, $100 groceries.

Rita: Aug 13, $385: $150 mortgage, $100 gas, $100 groceries, $35 water.

Bob: Aug 15, $1,425: $500 mortgage, $220 gas, $100 prop tax, $60 house ins, $210 Life & Disability, $120 car ins, $210 groceries.

Rita: Aug 20, $385: $100 groceries, $120 wedding, $165 MC.

Rita: Aug 27, $385: $85 cable, $140 groceries, $55 telephone, $100 donations.

Bob: Aug 30, $1,425: $330 car pymt, $400 LOC, $400 big box, $100 hot water tank, $50 RESP, $125 misc.

September

Rita: Sept 3, $385: $200 mortgage, $80 hydro, $100 groceries.

Rita: Sept 10, $385: $150 mortgage, $100 gas, $100 groceries, $35 water.

Bob: Sep 15, $1,425: $500 mortgage, $220 gas, $100 prop tax, $60 house ins, $210 life & Disability, $120 car ins, $210 groceries.

Rita: Sept 17, $385: $100 groceries, $120 wedding, $165 MC.

Rita: Sept 24, $385: $85 cable, $140 groceries, $55 telephone, $100 donations.

Bob: Sept 30, $1,425: $330 car pymt, $400 LOC, $400 big box, $100 hot water tank, $50 RESP, $125 misc.

Balances at 3 months

MC(Mastercard)- $5,114.00

LOC(Line of Credit)- $1,900.00

Big Box card- $220.00

Savings at 3 months

RESP(registered education savings plan)- $150.00

Hot water tank- $300

Wedding- $460.00

October

Rita: Oct 1, $385: $200 mortgage, $100 groceries, $80 hydro.

Rita: Oct 8, $385: $150 mortgage, $100 gas, $100 groceries, $35 water.

Bob: Oct 15, $1,425: $500 mortgage, $220 gas, $100 prop tax, $60 house ins, $210 life & disability, $120 car ins, $210 groceries.

Rita: Oct 15, $385: $85 cable, $55 telephone, $140 groceries, $100 donations.

Rita: Oct 22, $385: $100 groceries, $120 wedding, $165 MC.

Rita: Oct 29, $385: $200 big box, $100 wedding, $80 MC.

Bob: Oct 31, $1,425: $330 car pymt, $220 big box, $280 LOC, $25 RESP, $345 wedding, $125 misc, $100 hot water tank.

November

<u>Rita: Nov 5, $385</u>: $200 mortgage, $100 groceries, $80 hydro.

<u>Rita: Nov 12, $385</u>: $150 mortgage, $100 groceries, $100 gas, $35 water.

<u>Bob: Nov 15, $1,425</u>: $500 mortgage, $220 gas, $100 prop tax, $60 house ins, $120 car ins, $210 life & disability, $210 groceries.

<u>Rita: Nov 19, $385</u>: $85 cable, $55 telephone, $140 groceries, $100 donations.

<u>Rita: Nov 26, $385</u>: $100 groceries, $285 MC.

<u>Bob: Nov 30, $1,425</u>: $330 car pymt, $800 LOC, $100 hot water tank, $125 misc, $50 RESP.

December

Rita: Dec 3, $385: $200 mortgage, $100 groceries, $80 hydro.

Rita: Dec 10, $385: $150 mortgage, $100 groceries, $100 gas, $35 water.

Bob: Dec 15, $1,425: $500 mortgage, $220 gas, $100 prop tax, $60 house ins, $210 life & disability, $120 car ins, $210 groceries.

Rita: Dec 17, $385: $85 cable, $55 telephone, $100 donations, $140 groceries.

Bob Bonus Dec 21: $800: $600 Christmas, $200 MC.

Rita: Dec 24, $385: $100 groceries, $280 MC.

Bob: Dec 31, $1,425: $330 car pymt, $820 LOC, $25 RESP, $125 misc, $100 hot water tank.

Rita: Dec 31, $250 (reduced for holiday time off)- $250 MC.

Year End Balances

Owing

Big Box Card: 0

LOC: 0

Master Card: $3,849

Savings

Wedding: Paid in full with cash

Hot water tank: $600 ready to purchase

RESP: $250.00

Six months and these folks have worked hard to make their short term goals come true and pay off the debts with the highest interest rates. Notice that Bob and Rita did not take the nice vacation in the summer, they made their choice to work so that they could attend a wedding.

The year ahead looks good for them with the

Mastercard debt chopped down and ready to be eliminated within 3 to 4 months. They can then begin saving for retirement on a monthly basis.

NOTES